THE COLLEGE PRECIPICE
Faith and Life for Young Women

Anna L. Davis

xulon
PRESS

The College Precipice
Faith and Life for Young Women

by Anna L. Davis

Printed in the United States of America

ISBN 978-1-60477-846-5

www.xulonpress.com

Dedication

To Brad.

On campus, in the suburbs, and wherever else life takes us – I have loved and will love you there. Thank you for believing in me.

Table of Contents

𝄫

Acknowledgements

I began work on this manuscript late one night several years ago. Brad and the kids had already fallen asleep, and I couldn't settle down, so I pulled out the laptop and began to write, just babbling my thoughts onto the screen. And to my surprise I found myself writing this book. How it gripped me! It felt as though God Himself shook the words out of me. Then when the writing and publishing process became difficult, God used the people in my life to support me.

I would like to thank the women from Greenville Oaks Church of Christ who contributed their thoughts to this project. For our small group, and all my friends in Friday-morning Ladies Bible Study, thank you for lifting me up in prayer (and watching the kids) during these last few years. Thank you, Katelyn Reed, for your valuable input while editing this manuscript during your own early college years.

I would also like to thank all of my family, both immediate and extended. To the Barber side, your continual support of my goals throughout my life has given me the courage to accomplish them. To the Straley/Pugh side, thank you for encouraging me – knowing and loving you has been a blessing. And to the Davis side, thank you for accepting me so readily into your family – I can't imagine my life without you now.

To all of you who took time to ask me about the book's progress – thank you. You will never know how much that simple gesture encouraged me to keep striving toward publication.

Chapter 1. Standing at the Edge

Teach me to do your will, for you are my God; Let your good Spirit lead me on level ground. Psalm 143:10

I couldn't help but think of a pirate plank as I climbed the ladder toward a wooden platform, suspended about eight feet off the ground in mid-air. Half-expecting to hear the guide call me "matey," I paused for a moment, only to hear the familiar chatter of high school classmates below, and a serene rustling of leaves above.

I knew what to do – several of my friends had just done this – so I walked to the end of the platform, looked out across a sea of friends, then turned around, my back toward my classmates, facing the guide. At this point I began to feel frightened. What if it didn't work? "On the count of three," she began. "One... two... three!"

With a rush of adrenaline I fell backwards, into the arms of people with whom I had shared my teenage years. Working as a team to keep my body elevated – mosh-pit style – they carried me to the end of the group and set me down feet first, perfectly exemplifying what we had come to learn – that trust and teamwork get the job done.

At the time I thought it strange that we would go to a team-building ropes course for our senior trip, since people usually do something like this at the beginning of a project, rather than as a form of goodbye. Of course, we had tons of fun (most of which included staying up all night and shaving cream ambushes). But we already knew how to work as a team – four years of high school activities had done that.

Little did I know, though, how accurately this event fore-shadowed the coming first year of college. Sure, the param-eters changed – the stakes became higher. But when it came right down to it, going forward into life and leaving the past behind was really just another test of trust – both thrilling and frightening at the same time.

A precipice is[1]: 1) a cliff with a vertical, nearly vertical, or overhanging face, and 2) a situation of great peril. Going to college can be a huge precipice in your life by both defi-nitions. Here you stand, on relatively secure ground (while acknowledging that every woman comes from a different background, I use the word secure because this reality is *known*) – overlooking a giant chasm beyond which sits the new reality – your ideal adult life.

This precipice can be emotional or physical, but it always holds a spiritual dimension. Separating your faith from that of your parents and friends, learning to depend on God for big answers to life decisions, deciding which path to take – these things test you – they test your spirit, your resolve, your faith, your strength. Trusting God during these tests takes you into adulthood with tremendous potential. But I'm not talking about the scholastic potential that high school counselors dangle before you almost like bait, as in "you have great potential if you just apply yourself." I mean real faith potential – real faith *energy* – that takes you through the trials of life, which gives you peace when everything else falls apart.

This may sound poetic and all, but how does it actually work? That's why we're here together on these pages – to acknowledge that early womanhood can be a time of crisis and to learn that God will get you through it. This isn't a solution book as for calculus – I can't say that if you do A and B, the result will be C. Only God knows your individual formula for getting through the college precipice. I hope that you see me as a friend along your journey – a friend who has been over (and into) the precipice, and can therefore help guide you toward His hands.

It won't be easy at times. Not because Jesus Himself makes it difficult, but because we all have so many other hands vying for our touch. Have you ever tried to hold two hands with your one? What about three? It's possible to grip one hand with your pinkie finger, another with your pointer finger, and so on. But when push comes to shove, the hand that tries to hold many other hands will lose its grip on all of them. The strongest bond results when your one hand intertwines with someone else's one hand, with the fingers fitting together.

Like a suitor fighting away the hands of other men, God can use your early adult years to separate you from parents, friends, boyfriends, goals, sin, ideals, anything that gets in the way of your relationship with Him. When God calls you away from childhood friends who turned down the wrong path, when He shows you the shortcomings of your parents' faith, when He turns your goals upside down as you search for the life you want (yet also the life God has planned for you) – these events bring pain and separation from the people you love, and loss from letting go.

This same principle applies when you move away from home. You face a spiritual dimension of leaving home that your non-Christian friends don't understand. It's a paradox of sorts – you're breaking away from all that you've known, while simultaneously trying to remain close to Christ, even though He is often associated with the very things from which you try to separate yourself.

For example, you may have worshipped at church with friends and family while growing up, prayed with them at meals, and sought their advice on spiritual development. But at some point, Jesus Himself beckons you away from your family and friends. Come with Me. Depend on Me alone. Trust Me. And He opens the door of your parent's home, calling you outside.

This can be a precious moment in your spiritual life; but it can also be extraordinarily difficult if you have trouble separating your own faith from your hometown church or the faith of your parents. This breaking away process, with its good and bad, is vital to your Christianity – it's part of the precipice.

In Biblical times, young girls lived in their father's house and transitioned into their husband's house, usually without a time of independence in between. They probably experienced a precipice before marriage, as they took on the role of wife. And while modern women certainly face a marriage precipice, most women today encounter their first big faith-jump during the college and early adult years, when our society gives young women countless pre-marriage choices.

Have you Decided on a Major (Life)?

At a time when most 18 to 20 year old women struggle to cope with the spiritual and emotional dimensions of leaving home, our culture also calls upon you to begin making gigantic decisions about the overall course of your life.

This may seem overly dramatic. But think about it – most colleges give students about two years to choose a major. Once you have chosen a major, it follows naturally to think about a career path. But in choosing a career, you must also take into consideration your long-term life goals.

Will you need an advanced degree? Will advanced education delay having a family? Do you want to have a family? If so, when? And then what happens to your career once you have children? Do you go back to work, or stay at home? Will your chosen career field allow you to take a child-rearing hiatus? Or will a few years out of the loop be your professional undoing?

This doesn't even begin to skim the surface of other co-existing pressures, like parental expectations to go into a certain field. And then there's also the question of what God wants for your life.

Most people approach God's will for their life as some big mystery. It seems forever elusive, this God-ordained future that will make everything else fall into place. And then you go to school or interview for a job, and because of this elusiveness you feel totally alone in planning your future. Stress builds up within you – am I doing what God wants for me? How will these decisions affect my future family? We'll talk about these concerns in detail, and discuss how to have faith in God's ability to carve out your ideal earthly life.

Grr-l, Goddess, or Godly

Just for fun, take a minute to consider the quotes with which you most strongly agree.

- My first job is to be a good mother. (Faye Dunaway, actress)
- Be it unto me as You have said. (Mary, Mother of Jesus)
- Madonna is my role model – she's such a powerful woman. (Kirsten Dunst [in 1982], actress)
- I love you, but I love myself more. (Samantha Jones, Sex and the City character)
- A career is wonderful, but you can't curl up with it on a cold night. (Marilyn Monroe, actress)
- People think at the end of the day that a man is the only answer to fulfillment. Actually a job is better for me. (Princess Diana, British icon)

When researching these quotes, I learned something about womanhood: there's probably as many different ideas of what being a woman means, as there are women. Here's the strange part – during the next few years and into your twenties, you will probably choose from among these ideas what kind of woman you want to become, and you will almost certainly struggle to see your own clear path through all the overgrowth.

For example, we know that Christ teaches humility and self-sacrifice, direct opposites of ambition and self-involvement. But wouldn't you agree that getting ahead in the business world demands a certain degree of self-promotion, especially for women? As another example, we know in our hearts that God created women to be different from men, that He gave us certain attributes that men don't possess, and vice versa. Acknowledging these differences in our culture today, though, will bring you some dirty looks at best, a lawsuit at worst.

And once you discover for yourself what it means to be a woman, then you need to decide how to handle these womanly qualities from a Christian worldview. But again, finding this path might be difficult, because so many opinions exist even within Christian churches about women. Female church leadership is probably the most prominent example, as some denominations see no problem with women elders and others interpret the Bible as saying that church leaders should be male only. But let's look at something closer to your own life.

When faced with a challenge like finding a job or competing with classmates, do you feel like you should 1) work hard by your own standards, 2) work harder because you're a woman, or 3) back down and let the men do it? This is essentially an argument about "can" and "should" – *can* women perform well alongside other women and men, and *should* women choose to compete?

Can **We?** Of course, we say quickly. But the numbers tell us that we think something else: studies show that women in Christian colleges struggle with issues of personal confidence[2], while by contrast women at secular colleges have actually become more confident. But even women at secular colleges still rank behind men in this area.

So this means that if you put a bunch of college-aged men and women in the same room and give them some type of challenging task, more women than men will doubt their ability to complete the task. If you fill the room up with only women and give them a challenging task, more women who attend Christian colleges will feel incompetent compared to those who go to state school, for instance.

This doesn't say good things about us, ladies.

Should **We?** According to the Council for Christian Colleges and Universities (CCCU), most women graduating from Christian colleges earn degrees in education, health sciences, or social sciences, and nearly one-third end up with careers in education[3]. This doesn't really mean much of anything until you compare it with this fact: women tend to change their focus during college, with more women majoring in social sciences than originally thought they would as first-year students, and fewer women majoring in health sciences than originally thought they would. The authors of this study speculate that Christian women "are continuing to choose 'traditional' majors such as these for a host of reasons," one of which is that "these majors appear child-friendly." And thank God, because we need good Christian teachers (and mothers) in this world.

But this brings us to our point: *should* a Christian woman make the sacrifices necessary to move ahead in the professional world? Now we're getting into the heart of the Christian female identity crisis. (I'm not implying here that teachers have it easy in the sacrifice department. The authors of this study note that seemingly child-friendly careers like teaching actually require much more time than women realize.)

We'll talk more about this later.

Party Time

This is college! So of course you want to have fun – but what kind of fun? As a Christian, you've ruled out sinful fun. Or have you? When you've been studying all day, dealing with the pressures of this new world, which sounds more appealing – a quiet, focused Bible study, or a loud and unassuming pa-rrr-tey? And while some of your peers will make it through this time without giving in to sinful pressure, many who go to secular colleges (even Christian colleges) dabble in underage drinking, partying, and sex. Our culture celebrates these decisions – it views partying as part of independence, part of growing up.

Studies show that 70 percent of all college students drank alcohol in the past month[4]. According to sources cited by the National Institute on Alcohol Abuse and Alcoholism, "alcohol consumption on many campuses has evolved into a rite of passage. Traditions and beliefs handed down through generations of college drinkers serve to reinforce students' expectations that alcohol is a necessary component of social success."[5]

While we can argue that even Christian women need to sow their wild oats, these decisions inevitably bring consequences, like confusion, pain, and guilt, which could separate you from God and make your life plans fuzzy. Maybe something like rape changes your life forever[6]. Or maybe guilt takes hold and keeps you from going to church, from praying, from joy in Christ.

Soaring over Your Precipice

I think you're probably getting the picture. The precipice you face during early college has long-lasting, even eternal implications – it's a time of confusing choices, danger and temptation. And in returning to our earlier definition, you will indeed find yourself within a situation of great peril. Professional, social, emotional, and spiritual successes seemingly hang on your every decision. But it can also be a time of unprecedented spiritual understanding, a time when you learn what Jesus means to you personally.

I want to close this chapter with a look at Matthew 8:23-26. I think the message comes through so clearly that further elaboration would only add words without meaning.

Then He got into the boat and His disciples followed Him. Without warning, a furious storm came up on the lake, so that the waves swept over the boat. But Jesus was sleeping. The disciples went and woke Him, saying, "Lord, save us!

We're going to drown!" He replied, "You of little faith, why are you so afraid?" Then He got up and rebuked the winds and the waves, and it was completely calm.

Chapter 2. A Bittersweet Reality: Leaving "Home"

You never will finish being a daughter… You will be on when you're ninety and so will I. Gail Godwin

Leaving home represents a rite of passage – the ending of childhood, as you mature into an adult. Though this seems obvious, most people don't fully get it until their mid-twenties, if even then. Don't believe me? Then check out your local bookstore for an entire genre about the phenomenon known as "quarterlife crisis" – a period in the lives of twenty-something college graduates in which they wonder: "who am I," "why am I here," and "how do I navigate life?"

Answering these questions should begin way before the mid-twenties. And while such thoughts may linger beyond college, leaving home is a crucial step in defining your adulthood – a step that begins right now.

We leave home in three different ways: physically, emotionally, and spiritually. You're probably up to your ears in information about dorm life, money management, laundry control, and setting your own limits – the physical side of leaving home. But in addition to these physical realities, you also need to make emotional adjustments. We all know people who, despite living on their own, continue to depend on their parents for emotional nurturing on a regular basis. While we will do this for the rest of our lives in some respects, as we grow older we must learn to nurture ourselves and accept parental nurturing as more of a blessing than a necessity.

Beyond this, I'll leave the physical and emotional difficulties of leaving home to the countless books that are available for young adults and parents alike as they cope with changing roles during the college years.

Instead I want to look at the spiritual side of leaving home.

Leaving Home Spiritually (Without Leaving Your Spiritual Home)

God calls you into a deeper relationship with Him, a relationship that's separate from your relationship with your parents. In this sense, you will leave home spiritually with dozens of small choices that differentiate you from parental expectations. Let's think about some ways that you might differentiate yourself spiritually:

o Deciding to attend church with a different denomination
o Going to a more/less progressive version of your hometown church
o Being more/less involved in church than your parents
o Questioning the authenticity of your parents' faith
o Depending on God's goodness more (and parental, human goodness less)
o Developing a more diligent prayer time
o Listening more closely for God's guidance above all others

In addition to these small choices along the way, leaving home can also happen dramatically, as when God calls you to take a break from classes for a semester to better focus on Him. Just try telling your parents that God wants you to drop out of school for a while, and see how they react. With drama, I'm sure!

These things must be God-led, rather than out of rebellion. Leaving home spiritually happens when you follow God's pull within you, not because you need to be different from your parents, but because you want to be like Him. How will you know the difference?

Let's take worship style as an example. Do you feel called to worship differently from your parents; does worship flow from your heart differently? When you worship in this new way, do you feel an unmistakable connection with God? Does this style of worship agree with biblical guidelines? Then it might be possible that God wants you to worship differently from your parents, not to be different, but to have a more personal relationship with Him. It should probably go without saying that a "holier than thou" attitude about these changes misses the point.

As you begin to seek and act on God's will, people in your life may react negatively, not out of disapproval, really, but because they need time to catch up.

We all have expectations of loved ones. Your family has certain expectations of you based on your life with them at home. They understand the "you" who lived with them – the you who had certain goals, who lived life a certain way. But if God calls you toward different goals – if He changes your focus to bring you closer to His own plan, then your parents, like you, may struggle with the change.

The Jesus Who Left Home

Fortunately, the Bible provides a solid model for parent-adult interactions. Let's look at three verses from Jesus' life after He became a man, which give insight into what it means to leave home spiritually.

A Shocking Request. *And everyone who has left houses or brothers or sisters or father or mother or children or fields for my sake will receive a hundred*

*times as much and will inherit eternal life. But many
who are first will be last, and many who are last will
be first.* Matthew 19:29-30.

In Biblical times, families stayed together. A person's
entire reputation could rest on the name of her family – family
names followed people throughout life. Women, especially,
lived in their father's house until they married, from which
point they lived with and served their husbands.

I want you to separate yourself, for the moment, from
modern day America. Imagine that you have grown up in
your parents' home during the first century, A.D. One day
you go to the well for water, and there sits the Son of God
Himself. Jesus simply says "Follow Me," and everything
changes from that moment. How would your parents feel?
How would you feel, for that matter? What about your childhood friends, maybe a longtime boyfriend? What about your
own dreams?

Let's return to modern times. Jesus has called you away
from your home and said "Follow Me." Through prayer, you
must make yourself open to what God wants for your life;
from the moment you became a Christian, to the moment you
die, to all of eternity – following Jesus means everything.

Focused on a Purpose. *While Jesus was still talking
to the crowd, his mother and brothers stood outside,
wanting to speak to him. Someone told him, "Your*

27

mother and brothers are standing outside, wanting to speak to you." He replied to him, "Who is my mother, and who are my brothers?" Pointing to his disciples, he said, "Here are my mother and my brothers. For whoever does the will of my Father in heaven is my brother and sister and mother." Matthew 12:46-50.

We've already talked about the importance of family during Jesus' culture and this verse remains consistent – the "someone" in this verse expected Jesus to stop teaching and make time for his earthly family. In a way, our culture expects this same thing. Even in the Christian circle we often place earthly families above church family – after all, blood is thicker than water, as we say.

Jesus has a different message for disciples like you – doing God's will has more priority than keeping up with your family of origin. In this passage, Jesus felt that God wanted Him to teach the multitudes at that time, and he did not want to be distracted. He didn't allow earthly ties (precious as these may be) to keep Him from heavenly goals.

As a mother of two young children, I am learning how much work – how much of myself – goes into parenting; therefore part of me has a strange reaction to the passage above – indignation. After all, didn't Mary and her other sons deserve more attention than the "multitude"? Didn't they deserve something more than "who are My mother and brothers" – maybe some kind of formal introduction, at least? I wonder if Mary went home that evening and filled Joseph's ears with rants about ungrateful children (probably not, but Scripture doesn't include her response so I can't help but wonder).

In the same way, your family may have trouble when you decide to give God and your spiritual family first priority – we're all human, after all. But Jesus sends a clear message here – God comes first, even before parents.

> **Love and Honor.** *Near the cross of Jesus stood his mother, his mother's sister, Mary the wife of Clopas, and Mary Magdalene. When Jesus saw his mother there, and the disciple whom he loved standing nearby, he said to his mother, "Dear woman, here is your son," and to the disciple, "Here is your mother." From that time on, this disciple took her into his home. Later, knowing that all was now completed, and so that the Scripture would be fulfilled, Jesus said, "I am thirsty." John 19:25-28.*

Notice towards the end of this passage, that it says "after this, Jesus, knowing that all things had already been accomplished." After what? Only *after* Jesus found a surrogate son to care for his mother did He know all things had been accomplished.

Does this strike you as strange? The man who called His followers to leave home, who didn't take time to speak with his mother while teaching the multitude, who while teaching placed more importance on His eternal family than on His mother and brothers – this same man now uses a precious few dying words to provide for His earthly mother. And more than that, He sees these words – this act – as part of His mission.

It's important to clarify this issue, because like myself, you have probably become so ingrained in our culture that leaving home almost always goes hand in hand with self-centeredness and ungratefulness. Teenagers often rebel and draw away from their parents – our society celebrates their courage for "finding themselves." Young adults go away to college and never look back, forging ahead into the work force – our society applauds this as "growing up."

Perhaps due to our history, American culture values hard work and hard-won independence over family ties and obligations. Just a moment ago we talked about how as a culture we prioritize earthly family over spiritual family. So our cultural priority list might look like this: 1) Me, 2) Family, 3) God and Spiritual Family.

And yet Jesus calls you to a better attitude. This brings us to the final point of this chapter.

Honor Commandment Meets College

Honor your father and your mother, that your days may be prolonged in the land which the LORD your God gives you. Exodus 20:12.

Clearly, when you lived at home, certain things fell into the "honoring parents" category. Wash the dinner dishes, obey curfew, no talking on the phone past 10 pm – these rules gave you the opportunity to honor your parents by honoring their requests. But what now? How does "honor your father and mother" translate to the college campus?

I need to be honest with you before we move into this section. God has blessed me with two mothers, each with their own unique roles in my life. Inherent in this blessing is His command to honor them both, along with my dad. I didn't always understand this, but I am grateful for this understanding now. I still mess up, though. In fact, the other morning after editing this chapter, my birthmother and I had a disagreement over the phone. The words I chose to use certainly didn't convey honor; my tone even less so. Feeling like a hypocrite, I briefly considered removing this section completely and referring you to a different source.

But then I realized something – you need to know about my struggle. Ladies, college is just the beginning of a changing relationship with your parents. And you won't always get it right, nor will they. Long past college graduation the dance will continue, and at times they will hurt you or pull you too close, and other times you will step on their toes or push them too far away. Even so, the honor commandment remains in effect.

So that brings us back around to our question – how do you honor your parents once you leave home? Let's look at five ways.

1) **Consideration.** At this point in your life, you probably don't want to need anyone, especially not your parents. You want to prove to them and to yourself that you're an adult. But when we honor someone, we also care what he or she thinks. That's why we yell out "speech, speech!" when someone receives an award: we want to hear what this honored person has to say. It's the same with parents – honoring them means we consider their thoughts.

2) **Gratitude.** For a job well done, even for your very existence – being thankful for your parents honors them greatly. You can be straightforward with your thankfulness, as in a thank-you note or heartfelt Father's Day card. Or it can be more subtle, as part of your conversation. Just make sure the message gets across.

3) **Prayer.** Your parents also face a precipice, especially if they now live in an empty nest. Pray for your relationship with them, as you both transition into this new reality. When you feel annoyed or angry with them, pray immediately. If you have trouble showing gratitude and giving them consideration, at the very least you can pray for them.

4) **Personal Responsibility.** Take responsibility for your own actions. Many parents consider a self-sufficient,

functional adult to be one of the greatest honors of parenthood. Of course – you will need to consider the advice of others, especially those people who know you well. You should still listen carefully to your parents and glean wisdom from their experience. They likely have your best interests at heart, as they did when you were under their wing. But growing up means that your successes and failures suddenly become your own responsibility, your own choices.

5) **New Boundaries.** Respectfully set boundaries for your new adult-parent relationship – the key word being "respectfully." Establish with your parents the importance of having your own place and planning your own time (within reason, of course). Some parents may already respect your boundaries, and you might not need to consciously set new ones. Other parents might have trouble in this area. Your boundaries will be specific to your relationship with them.

Take Kelly, for example.

"My most difficult adjustment was the first summer home from college after my freshman year," she says. "I had spent that year learning to live on my own (within the boundaries of dorm life and curfews) and make my own decisions. I was suddenly back home under their roof and their rules."

After "butting heads" for a while, Kelly and her parents had a talk that resulted in respectful boundaries all around.

On her end, Kelly learned that she needed to respect her parents' space in the way they wanted to run their own home.

"Basically it came down to: I was back in their house and living there meant more than having room and board," she says. "I was still an active, participating member of the family and I owed them the common courtesies of telling them where I was going, when I would be back, and negotiating a return time."

On their end, Kelly's parents learned to let go a little more.

"During our discussion, Mom did recognize that I had changed and I had been making my own decisions and she was willing to give me more flexibility if I was willing to keep them in the loop," Kelly says. "Once we both adjusted our expectations, the summer went a lot more smoothly."

Chapter 3. Dream Deep:
Leaving "Own"

🦋

Reach high, for stars lie hidden in your soul. Dream deep, for every dream precedes the goal. Pamela Vaull Starr

Since Judy Garland as Dorothy looked in wonder upon the land of Oz, the phrase "Toto, I've a feeling we're not in Kansas anymore" has been repeated to describe anything strange and life-altering, and this category certainly includes college. For those of you familiar with this movie, how did Dorothy end up in Oz in the first place?

She bumped her head during a tornado, fell unconscious, and began to dream.

You've probably heard a lot about dreams lately. Follow your dreams. Hold fast to your dreams. Dreaming about the future has great rewards, because by dreaming you discover what you want in life. In some ways your dreams distinguish you from every other high school graduate entering college

– nobody will ask about your high school GPA or SAT score (at least not after the first week) – instead they will ask about your major, about what you want to do with life, about your dream.

But as with Dorothy's adventures in Oz, sometimes dreams can take you into unusual places, potentially altering your entire outlook on life. Sometimes dreams will hide for a while, camping out in your subconscious while you struggle to choose a major. And sometimes, in fact oftentimes, dreams may change.

In an Oz-like moment, you may find yourself separated from this aspect of your identity, *your dream*; and as college whirls around you, pulling and pushing in every direction, you wonder what happened to the *you* who had it all figured out, who knew where you wanted to go and how to get there.

The Dream

I believe that your dream – defined here as aspiration, goal, or aim – comes directly from God in abstract form, as a way to use your unique gifts and talents He gave you, and only you. The Dream in itself says nothing about how or when; it merely exists within your mind and heart, waiting to be realized.

What do you feel passionate about? What do you *want* to do with life? Chances are that your dream lingers somewhere within your answers– but notice that I didn't say your dream equates to your answers. Life has a way of caging your dream into neat, tidy packages. "I want to be a doctor, so I can help people," for example, when the dream within can really be boiled down to: "I want to help people." And there's lots of ways to help people beyond the health sciences.

We often associate dreams with ambition. Strictly speaking, they mean the same thing, but they have different connotations. "Dream" implies something lofty, almost fanciful, while "ambition" seems self-advancing, stopping at nothing to get ahead. So which would you rather be: lofty and fanciful, or self-advancing and driven? Head in the clouds, or nose to the grindstone? "I want to help people," versus "I will go to medical school after graduating magna cum laude from an Ivy League university."

Clearly your personality type plays a major role in shaping your dreams, but somewhere inside of you, beyond personality constraints and circumstantial challenges, a dream continues to exist.

The Plan

Right now dreaming may be synonymous with planning. Countless relatives and teachers have asked: so what do you want to do with your life? What's your plan? And you've answered them, the same answer for at least a dozen people. After all, they want to know what kind of young adult you will become. So it doesn't seem appropriate to answer: I want to write, or I want to help people, or whatever. That doesn't seem *defined* enough. And so at some point you begin to believe that you must have a plan in place before the dream means something. In reality, though, it's the other way around.

But in no way does this mean that you shouldn't plan – we all know that anything of value comes from planning and hard work: winning the Nobel Prize, wearing an Olympic gold medal or developing a cure for cancer, for example. Even the less tangible goals require a plan. If I want to become a more caring person, then I would plan to call my friends and family more often to keep up with their lives and perhaps I would plan to send letters of encouragement regularly through mail or email. People who accomplish great things in life – who effect positive self-change and live out their dreams – must have a plan.

Notice the last two words of the previous sentence: *a* plan. Not *The Plan*. What's the difference? A plan exists as a guideline; The Plan makes no allowances for flexibility. A plan shows humility; The Plan reflects arrogance – that you know best. A plan leaves room for God; The Plan easily becomes a thing of ownership.

For God to grow The Dream in your life, He needs to work within the flexible guidelines of a plan that you've created. Only God knows the outcome of The Dream. If by some chance you've tied your heart to The Plan, two things could happen: 1) you rigidly carry out The Plan, potentially missing what God really wants to accomplish through The

Dream He gave you, or 2) God will ask you to release ownership of The Plan.

God-*Driven* Dreams

"Why is a daisy always a daisy? Because it cooperates
with the Creator in being what He made it to be. It glori-
fies God. George Mueller said in a message he preached in
Dublin, Ireland, "Friends, how many objectives do you have
in life? Three? Then you have two too many! Two? Then
you have one too many! One, and that *one the glory of God*?
Then you are like your Master!" Keeping that one goal in
mind, we can change the most commonplace things of life
into treasures to lay at the Master's feet.

True spirituality on an individual basis is cooperating
with God, moment by moment, in becoming what He meant
for you to be, thus glorifying Him and being a blessing to
Him. When this is so, you will naturally be a blessing to
others."

— *Keeping Your Balance: A Woman's Guide to
Physical, Emotional, and Spiritual Well-Being* [12]

We can take a perfectly good, God-*given* dream and turn
it into a cookie-cutter life filled with moments of regret. It's
like the game you played in elementary school called "tele-
phone", where one person passes a message to a classmate
beside her and on down the line, and eventually the original

message gets completely distorted. We humans can really mess up God's messages.

While I firmly believe that our dreams for the future come directly from God, I also believe that we often think inside the box of our own plans for achieving those dreams. And at some point God says to let it go. We can fight it, we can say it's mine – my dream, my plan, my life! We can ignore His voice, His nudge.

Or we can let Him control the dream, and look in wonder at what happens next. But allowing God to control this part of your life requires that you let go of your own plan, not necessarily in action (though sometimes this will be the case), but in terms of your emotional commitment.

Letting Go

Jamie met her future husband during freshman year at Abilene Christian University.

"He was a senior when I was a freshman and he is the same age as my older brother. They were in the same fraternity and were good friends. He did the 'dating his friend's little sister thing'," Jamie says.

By *her* senior year, they had become engaged. This fit in with most of her life plan, because Jamie definitely wanted to share her life with someone within marriage and start a family someday.

But this decision to settle down didn't agree well with the rest of her life plan – to become a lawyer.

I was a political science/pre-law degree with plans of attending law school," she says. "My husband was older than me and had already established his mortgage company here in Dallas. If I was going to live here then I would have to go to law school here."

Thinking about the realities of law school led Jamie to one startling conclusion.

"By the time I finally finished law school I would be ready to have kids and all that time and money would have gone to waste. I thought to myself that I could work for several years and then have kids, but I want to have my kids young."

She finally decided not to go to law school.

"During a time in my life when I wanted to be a lawyer it seemed like a huge decision," Jamie explains. "I know that God has great plans for me and he has provided me with a new job that I really like. I am going to have the flexibility to start my family when I am ready and not feel like I have wasted several years of my life."

Time and prayer let Jamie be in touch with the deeper dream of having a family. But letting go of her original plan – The Plan – initially caused some heartache, even though Jamie knew the best path.

Some of you may be feeling wary of this message right about now. Perhaps you plan to attend law school or medical school, and you feel like I'm devaluing this decision. I'm not. If you dream of becoming a lawyer or a doctor and this makes sense for your life, by all means go for it. And make a plan to get there! Just don't be afraid to look up every now and then, and ask "God, which way do *You* want me to go?"

> *Delight yourself in the Lord and He will give you the desires of your heart* (Psalms 37:4).

Chapter 4. Wild Oats and Oatmeal

❧

Be happy, young (wo)man, while you are young, and let your heart give you joy in the days of your youth. Follow the ways of your heart and whatever your eyes see, but know that for all these things God will bring you to judgment. Ecclesiastes 11:9 (parentheses mine).

True or false: Everybody parties in college.
Think hard about this. Really.
What do college students do for fun?

Of course, all kinds of answers exist for this question. The important factor here is your perception – what *you think* college students do for fun. This perception could be your driving force for good or harm as you seek recreation at college. If you perceive that college students have fun by attending college-organized events, then you will be likely to attend these events and enjoy them. On the other hand, if you think that college students party hard in true *Animal House* fashion, then fighting back those impulses might be the biggest challenge to your faith.

So before we elaborate, please take a moment to examine your perception.

Do you see your college-self going to Christian rock concerts with devoted friends? Attending regular Bible studies geared for your age group? Student union events? Eating pizza every day? Late-night study groups? Philosophical explorations?

Now be very honest with yourself. Do you long to let your hair down, to shed those pesky inhibitions? Somewhere, in the back of your mind, does college fun look like wild fraternity parties? Drinking until everything feels good? Dating the wrong kinds of guys? Sex? Drugs?

No, not me. I would never compromise my faith like that. And hopefully you won't. But we all have different degrees of temptation in our Christian life. Maybe for you, eating pizza everyday constitutes pretty hardcore partying, because you have a commitment to good health and don't want to gain weight. For others, going to a Christian rock concert might border on temptation – perhaps you dance suggestively, or flirt too much, or wear clothing that isn't really appropriate for a Christian concert. Maybe you don't like alcohol, but dating wild men usually becomes your downfall. Maybe you like *all* the bad stuff, and constantly work to keep these temptations under control. Maybe you've given in to them.

Perhaps you don't get into the typical party scene – you prefer intellectual debates instead of beer. Entertaining philosophical thoughts can actually strengthen your faith, if you use a Christian filter to reinforce your own beliefs. How? Well, as you learn new information in any class, look for God's presence in the material, using biblical principles to guide you. If God really created the universe and everything in it, then learning about our universe and the actions of humankind will tell you more about God. If you really believe that God is omniscient (all-knowing) and omnipotent (all-powerful), then everything in this earth can teach you about Him.

After all, nothing can negate truth – if Christianity is truth, then even anti-Christian ideas can prove Christianity. I personally found great strength in studying secular philosophy. To me, even the great anti-Christian thinkers ended up reinforcing my beliefs. But the problem comes when you make that one decision to accept an anti-Christian idea as possible in itself, and in that moment you begin sowing intellectual wild oats – a party of ideas, if you will. Once you see these ideas as possible, you begin to lose your spiritual footing.

In this chapter, we're going to look honestly at college partying and what it means for your spiritual life. This isn't a how-to guide about avoiding temptation, nor will this be a "don't drink, smoke, or date bikers" kind of diatribe. No, we're going to talk about something much more basic to the Christian faith: sin and redemption.

In fact, like Solomon in Ecclesiastes, I might even encourage you to follow the impulses of your heart. But know this: you can fight for your right to party, but God will continue to fight for your soul.

Dealing with Wild Oats

While the phrase *wild oats* historically describes unruly young men, I think it perfectly fits what also happens to young women in college: acting wild just for the sake of it. Living on the edge for no purpose, not as a means to an end in any way.

It's my belief that if wild oats are in your heart, they need to come out in order for you to grow closer to God. Somehow God will remove the sin (even the mere desire to sin) from your life. Praying in the face of temptation allows God to remove wild oats from your life, so that you don't even fall into sin. I'm finally at a point in my Christian journey where I trust God this much with my heart. That's not to say that I don't struggle with sin, but I hardly ever fall into willful sin anymore, and with God's grace maybe I won't ever again. But it hasn't always been this way.

Even after I became a Christian, I still struggled with willful, premeditated sin. God allowed me to fall into sin during college, so that He could remove it from me. We'll talk more about my own struggle during the next chapter, but right now, let's look together at ways to deal with the wild oats in your life.

Resist and Pray. As a Christian teenager, you undoubtedly faced temptation every day, probably even the very same temptations that you now face or soon will face in college. We usually accept that high school students should not drink, attend wild parties, and so on. But the line becomes more blurry in college.

Everybody parties in college. When does it become sin? So let's draw the line here: sin is sin, is sin. Drinking heavily? Sin. Underage drinking? Sin. Sex outside of marriage? Sin. Teasing guys, arousing their passions? Sin. Living in indulgence without respect for your body or the bodies of others? Sin.

I'm not here to judge you. Unfortunately, I know first hand the consequences of these sins. But don't lie to yourself when sin (in whatever form) confronts you. It may not look deadly, but Satan specializes in making sin seem subtle and enticing. If you trust God during this time you will become stronger in Him, and He will meet you there.

Sowing Wild Oats. We grow weary of resisting wild oat tendencies, or fail to even put up a fight. And so we give in to sin. At the most basic level, you probably just want to have fun. On a deeper level, you begin to act out the conflict within yourself, by sinning. In going back to an illustration from our previous chapter, we go from leaving home with Christ, to leaving home *and* Christ.

It all begins with a single decision. Maybe you think: what's the harm in one drink? This guy isn't right for me, but I'll just go out with him one time, just for fun. What's one little kiss? Sure, I'll go clubbing with you. Really, dancing like that doesn't mean anything.

Or you're sitting around with some friends, discussing philosophical "truths," when something like Nietzsche seeps into your brain, and you allow the thought to grow. Maybe God really is dead. Or maybe humans invented religion as a coping mechanism, to preserve our mental health. You know in your heart what the Bible says, but yet the thoughts remain. Wild oats of the mind can also be sinful.

God's Wonderful Paradox. Now, here's the catch. God can use your sin (the very thing that separates you from Him) to draw you closer to Him. Maybe you had unresolved wild oats in your heart, and the only way for God to remove those from you, is for you to sow them and reap the consequences. What consequences? Loss of direction, decline of health, confusion, and guilt, to name a few. When these consequences begin to eat at you, God will be there, waiting to welcome you home. It's your choice to go back.

When Oats Turn Into Oatmeal

First of all, I have nothing against oatmeal; it's a wonderfully healthy breakfast when seasoned with cinnamon and sugar (maybe even some dried fruit). But for our purposes, let's get real about oatmeal: it's mushy and bland. When you choose to sow your wild oats rather than resist temptation, you run the risk of becoming like oatmeal – spiritually mushy and bland. In Biblical terms, you reap what you sow.

You cannot sow wild oats for long before consequences surface. As my friend Ellie once said, "Don't lose God when you're trying to find yourself." If you have lost God during your own self-discovery process, you will have certain spiritual symptoms. You might become depressed, caught in a dark cycle of self-absorption and negativity. Anger might well up within you toward God, friends, and especially yourself. You'll feel lonely even though people surround you – but they just don't understand.

Spiritually, you'll feel like a hurricane swept your anchor away and now you're drowning. This will result in internal conflict from not acting as you believe, feelings of hypocrisy, guilt, and pain that results from separating yourself from God. If you've fallen into intellectual wild oats, your very core will be shaken terribly – you'll feel as though you've lost your center. I think this quote applies: "I used to have an open mind, but my brains kept falling out."

Other consequences might be confusion about your life path when you had previously understood God's plan for your life, declining grades, and a general "fuzziness" about life in general.

A Word about Sex. Here's the bottom line – if you happen to be a married college student, then have sex. If you're not married, though, sex falls into the broad category that we've called wild oats. The principles of resisting and/ or sowing apply directly to sex – ideally, resist and pray for guidance. Easier said than done. So please know that if you give into sexual desire before marriage, you will undoubtedly experience consequences.

As a woman, these consequences aim directly for your emotions, body image, and relationship security. You might become overly preoccupied with your appearance (vanity is the old-fashioned word for this), and worry about weight gain. You might develop insecurities about your relationship – does he think about other girls, past girlfriends? How did their bodies compare to yours? Did they do it better than you?

For more Christian thoughts about sex, check out *Real Sex: The Naked Truth about Chastity* by Lauren Winner.

Oatmeal vs. Normal Life Events

We need to clarify something here. I think that people who fall away from God to live a more liberal lifestyle will inevitably notice emotional and spiritual consequences. But I do not believe that people who suffer in some way must be suffering because of sin. Even believers who follow

Christ faithfully can experience depression, confusion, guilt, and even physical troubles. That's right – the Christian life doesn't mean that we'll be free from these things. So how can you tell the difference between wild oats consequences, and normal life troubles? In Matthew 7:16-20, Jesus says that we can know faithful believers by their fruits.

So let's look back at the fruits of the Spirit from Galatians 5:22 – love, joy, peace, patience, kindness, goodness, faithfulness, gentleness, and self-control. These qualities serve as a barometer of sorts for your Christian walk.

If you faithfully follow Christ, you will experience an increase in fruits of the Spirit. You may have more love, feel more kindness toward others, and so on. But if you have fallen into sin – backsliding, as church ministers call it – you will see a decline in your fruits of the Spirit. In fact, your thoughts and actions will reflect fruits of the flesh (sexual immorality, impurity, debauchery, idolatry and witchcraft; hatred, discord, jealously, fits of rage, selfish ambition, dissensions, factions and envy, drunkenness, orgies and the like – Galatians 5:19-21).

Your Choice

Once your life turns into oatmeal, you have two options: quit sinning and go back to God, or believe Satan's biggest lie.

Chapter 5. Guilt 101

๚

Running from the truth to protect my inner self, I have betrayed both God and the very self I tried to protect. Personal Journal, Sophomore Year

I went to a private Christian high school, and after a radical conversion shortly after my fifteenth birthday, I dove head-first into the Christian faith. Like many new Christians, I felt great zeal for reading the Bible, praying, and encouraging others in Christ. Going to a state college became a witnessing opportunity for me – look at all those lost souls who need God! This made it easy to say no to drinking parties across the hall – I had a higher purpose.

I truly felt that God called me to refrain from dating during freshman year, at least for a while. But then this one guy kept asking me out. I was flattered, but said no. And then one day, for some reason, I said yes. And that began about five months of dating a non-Christian guy, with whom I didn't really connect, just because he was a good companion for lonely times. I knew he was wrong for me in every sense, most importantly because God had said no.

I tried several times to break it off with him, but he was falling in love with me, and that love felt more appealing than loneliness. And the façade grew deeper – one night I had planned to break up with him once and for all, when he ended up taking me out to dinner with his parents. With his parents! Finally, after Christmas break I said it's over, stay away from me.

I can't tell you how worthless I felt in that moment. Not only had I sinned by not doing as God called me, but I had caused someone else pain because of it. I had become one of *those* women. That same day my neighbor invited me to a party at his apartment across the hall. And suddenly, there it was – my chance to escape, to be someone different than this person I had become.

I got drunk for the first time ever that night. Throughout the next semester, I went to numerous parties, learned how to play drinking games, and even hosted my own parties. Sins that had been dormant since my conversion to Christ came back again. How many nights did I stumble back to my own apartment, look at my blurry face in the mirror, and wonder what on earth had gotten into me?

Every time I even considered going to church or Bible study, I thought – what if someone there knew how much I partied last night? What if they call my bluff? And God knows, of course. He must be furious with me. This guilt held me in chains for that whole semester and quite some time after – it told me, you're not good enough, you're such a hypocrite, God doesn't want you anymore, you failed Him.

Satan's Best Lie to Believers

When we fall into sin, God longs to pick us up again. He wants to heal our souls, to fill up those empty spots with His love. And though this very concept within itself defines the Christian faith – Jesus died on the cross to forgive us – for some reason, something keeps us from going back to Him after we've sinned.

Guilt has several definitions, all related to some type of wrongdoing. We can say: 1) "I admit guilt," meaning yes, I did it; 2) "I feel guilty," meaning I feel bad about it; and 3) "I'm living a life of guilt," meaning that past wrongdoing has affected my daily life. The first and second definitions of guilt go along with confession and repentance. These types of guilt affect us briefly.

Chronic guilt – the third kind – results from unresolved feelings of wrongdoing. This type of guilt easily becomes a way of life, which turns into a terrible cycle that can only be the work of Satan himself, the great deceiver. Who else would condemn you in such a way, to keep you away from God?

So here's how guilt works. When you wake up on Sunday morning, memories of your actions the night before keep you from church – the very place you'll find healing. When somebody who knows that you're a Christian catches you in sin, you label her judgmental instead of admitting your sin and asking for prayer. When you feel lost and alone, you will do almost anything but pray, because like Adam and Eve in the garden after eating of the forbidden fruit, you want to hide from His holiness.

Emptiness develops within you – holes that God once filled with his love and peace become hollow. After enough time away from God, you begin to fill those holes with friends, activities, other obsessions. Soon you're entrenched in a life that's only a shadow of the one meant for you, bound to friends who keep you there, engaged in activities that reinforce your guilt.

If nothing stops this cycle, guilt fades into spiritual numbness. The faithful Christian life seems like fanaticism now; other hands vying for your attention push Jesus away. And you let it all happen, because you can't bear to go back to Him after what you've done. He probably won't accept you back anyway.

Or so Satan says.

Grace: The Antidote

Let's take one of the hypothetical situations we talked about earlier – guilt keeping you from church. But let's say that you do go to church, even though you stayed up partying until 3 am. You feel like the biggest hypocrite ever, and want to run out the door. But something keeps you there. And even though you did some horrible things last night, even though your hair stinks of cigarette smoke and beer, God Himself speaks to you. Awestruck by His presence, you silently ask for forgiveness. Jesus whispers directly into your ear "your sins are forgiven – go and sin no more." In a moment, grace trumps guilt.

We've already covered guilt and how it can affect your life. But grace ... well, I'll be honest with you by saying that most Christians, even lifelong believers, struggle with understanding grace. Simply stated, grace is God's unconditional love that played itself out when Jesus died on the cross. When you became a Christian, Jesus forgave all the sins you had ever committed. But what about the sins we commit after becoming Christians? Grace means that God continues to forgive these sins (assuming that we ask for forgiveness) because He loves us and sent His Son to die for this purpose.

Marcie grew up in a strong Christian family and regularly attended a close-knit country church. She knew the ABC's of the Christian faith inside and out – including grace – when she entered college. But nothing could prepare her for the pressures she faced as a freshman, and the guilt that soon followed.

"I turned to alcohol and dating too many non-Christian guys. It became more of an addiction than anything. The habitual sins were the hardest to get away from because not only was I acting against God's will; the guilt just kept adding up."

Marcie tried going to church, but she just found more party buddies there. Even through all of that, she says, "God never let go of me. I always pushed Him further and further away, but I could always feel Him."

"There's not a day that goes by that is not difficult for me to forgive myself for what I've done. It's not anything that I can change, just something I can learn from. I am still so very far from where God commands me to be. I have so many faults and errors, that I want to just stop trying."

"I can't though. I can't go back to where I was because *I know* I'll never be happy there. I give Him the responsibility of the nurturing and guidance, and hold to my responsibility to carry it out as best I can."

Thankfully, it isn't our job to forgive our own sins. We sang a song at church last week that perfectly captures this concept. I hope it touches your soul like it has mine.

> *When Satan tempts me to despair, and tells me of the*
>   *guilt within,*
> *Upward I look and see Him there, who made an end*
>   *to all my sin.*
> *Because the sinless Savior died, my sinful soul is*
>   *counted free.*
> *For God the Just is satisfied, to look on Him and*
>   *pardon me,*
> *To look on Him and pardon me[7].*

Chapter 6. Movin' On

So he got up and went to his father. "But while he was still a long way off, his father saw him and was filled with compassion for him; he ran to his son, threw his arms around him and kissed him. "The son said to him, 'Father, I have sinned against heaven and against you. I am no longer worthy to be called your son.'" Luke 15:20-21

We all know the story of the prodigal son, how he left home with his inheritance and then squandered it all on loose living. After he had spent everything, a famine swept the country. With all his fortune gone, he became so hungry that at one point he ate swine's food. At rock bottom, he decided to go home and ask for forgiveness. What happened next explains grace better than I ever could – his father saw him in the distance, ran to him, and embraced him.

I'm sure the meaning of this parable hits home with you. Wild oats, oatmeal, guilt and grace – all illustrated perfectly.

Before we end this section, though, we should look at one aspect of this story that the text doesn't fully mention – the road home.

Leaving the Oats Behind

What do you think the prodigal son thought about as he walked home? Maybe along the way, he encountered his favorite prostitute, and temptation beckoned him to her door. But he kept walking. Maybe he saw some of his drinking buddies, laughing it up at that friendly bar. So easy – much easier than going home to ask forgiveness. But he kept walking. When he saw his father on the horizon, maybe pride told him to turn and run back. But he kept walking.

And you must do the same. Going back to the Christian life after sowing your wild oats requires that you leave the oats behind. While living that life, you may have made some really great friends – probably good, fun people who partied with you. But unless they fully support your commitment to Jesus, you must leave them behind with the oats, at least for a while.

I know that this sounds highly intolerant, heresy in today's culture of pluralism. Our world values diversity of all kinds – spiritual diversity especially. And while there's nothing wrong with having friends who believe differently from you, the problem comes when you aren't strong enough to hold fast your own beliefs while tolerating theirs.

By its very nature, the road home wobbles with insecurity – Satan will do anything to keep you from returning to Christ, from entering back into His love. If you can manage to walk back toward Christianity while remaining close to party buddies, then pray your way through it and keep walking. But if they try to pull you back toward the swine, if you feel yourself leaning into that life again, keep walking without them.

Let's return to the parable. When the prodigal son walked home, passing by his former prostitutes and friends, what must these people have said to him? I'm sure they ridiculed him, mocking his attempts at a more spiritual life. They probably made him feel terrible for leaving them behind. In my own road back to Christianity, friends from the party life practically sneered at me – you're so traditional now, one friend said with a scowl. Another friend said, "but you're more enlightened than that." Other friends literally showed up at my doorstep with Jell-O shots. Maybe the most piercing comment came from my best friend when I wouldn't join her in that life anymore – "you weren't there for me when I needed you most." But had I stayed by her side, I might never have returned home.

In this way your road home may be difficult, but Jesus waits for you on the horizon – keep walking.

Looking Back

Today's churches spend a lot of energy encouraging their teens to avoid sin; youth programs focus heavily on college preparation to help graduating seniors recognize and avoid the spiritual pitfalls of college. I'm not criticizing this movement in any way. Hopefully these teens won't fall – they will pray their way through temptations and emerge stronger. But what happens if they do?

I fell into the precipice during freshman year of college, and God brought me out by the middle of sophomore year. Life got really busy after that – I became engaged, employed, and married – all before graduation. I didn't have time to process what falling into the precipice really meant for me, I just kept moving forward in my faith and in life.

Years later I found myself in a ladies Bible study called "Believing God," by Beth Moore. During one video session, Beth highlighted something she called "a sifting period," based on Luke 22:31-32:

> *"Simon, Simon, Satan has asked to sift you as wheat. But I have prayed for you, Simon, that your faith may not fail. And when you have turned back, strengthen your brothers."*

When we sift something, we separate the good parts that we want to keep from the unproductive or bad. In context, this verse takes place shortly before the crucifixion. Jesus, speaking to Simon (also named Peter), knows that Peter will soon deny Him three times.

Denying Christ isn't some circumstantial trial, like going through a death of a loved one; it's a willful insult to God's Son. Jesus Himself said that those who acknowledge Him before others, He will also acknowledge before His Father, those who disown Him, He will also disown (Matthew 10:32-33). Peter understood this, and yet he still denied knowing Christ. How great a sin for Peter!

Oh, and how a great a sin for you. After all, you knew the Truth before college. You knew what it felt like to walk with Him, talk with Him. You knew that others watch your every move for evidence of your Christianity, perhaps waiting to see you fail. Like Peter's, the words you prayed during high school ring hollow now, "I would never do that, Lord. I won't ever compromise." How great a sin!

I carried the above paragraph in my heart even after God forgave me. The sinful period during college had no purpose for me, except to remind me of my fallenness, of my capacity for sin, of my hypocrisy.

Until that one video session in ladies Bible study. Tears sprang to my eyes as God allowed His word to settle in my heart:

Satan sifted the sin to the top of my life, in hopes that it would remove God from me. God allowed this to happen, so that He could remove the sin.

God had control the whole time.

In addition to this sifting concept, four things from Luke 22 encourage me.

1. Satan asked Jesus for permission – he doesn't just get to mess with Christians unless God allows it.
2. In this case, Jesus allows Satan to sift Simon. We know that God always has a reason, and can very quickly use something for His purposes that Satan means for evil.
3. Jesus prayed for Simon's faith, as I believe He also prays for ours.
4. Jesus said "WHEN you have turned back, strengthen your brothers." Not if, when.

Clearly, Jesus didn't see Simon's denial/falling away as wasted time. He used it to refine and strengthen him for further service in the Kingdom.

Looking Forward

Not everyone will fall into the precipice – some women won't need to struggle with wild oats to further refine their faith. But for those of you who do fall, it's almost like hitting a pause button on your life. Until you fell into sin, your life probably carried forward momentum over the precipice of college and a full adult life. But then you fell, and you became preoccupied with sin itself and spiritual recovery from that sin. If this describes you, then please know that

God can use this time to complete wonderful things in your life. He's purifying you – removing from your spirit anything that keeps you from His arms.

Once you walk back to Him, your real life – the one you're meant to have – can begin again.

Chapter 7. Trusting God

To man belong the plans of the heart, but from the Lord comes the reply of the tongue. All a man's ways seem innocent to him, but motives are weighed by the Lord. Commit to the Lord whatever you do, and your plans will succeed. Proverbs 16:1-3

I love gymnastics, but I can't stand the vault. For those who aren't familiar with this event, gymnasts sprint toward a vault, jump off a springboard, and grab the vault with one or both hands. Then comes the fun part we see on TV, where Olympic gymnasts effortlessly approach the vault with great speed, flip over it gracefully, twirl through the air, and land feet-first on the mat (usually).

With that example in mind, I'll tell you about my girl-hood vaulting experience. I stared at the vault, thinking about what to do when I got there, going over the "plan" my coach laid out for me. Taking a deep breath, I ran toward the springboard, still with this "plan" in my head. My feet hit the springboard with great force, propelling me to the vault. So far, so good. My hands reached out to the vault, and then it happened. I became frozen by the idea of smashing into it – I couldn't complete the exercise! Awkwardly, painfully, I came to a complete standstill – the vaulting horse in front of me, unconquered.

Allow me to draw a loose metaphor with this vaulting example. You run through high school, admissions, tests, and orientation, jump off the springboard of leaving home, and suddenly you arrive with great momentum at college. Then what?

God Makes it Happen

At some point you might feel as though jumping over the precipice depends entirely on your own strength. Getting good grades, choosing a solid major, finding the perfect internship, getting involved in all the prestigious clubs, making positive friends, dating the perfect guy – these things rest on your shoulders.

Many college-aged women feel this way. Even Christian women who understand God's sovereignty struggle with this weight-of-the-world mentality. According to studies from the Council for Christian Colleges and Universities, more women than men feel overwhelmed by all that they have to do, including studying, finding a job, working for pay, and volunteering. While men also do many of these things, they are less likely to worry about it to the point of feeling overwhelmed.

Why do we as women have so much trouble letting go? I come from a long line of worry-ers, including my grandmother. When something bad happens in my family, we have in the past agreed not to tell Grandma, because it would only cause her to worry. One day she told me that she would rather worry than be in the dark. Not knowing what was happening when clearly everyone else knew caused her even more worry than not worrying about the particular issue. I didn't understand this at all, until just recently when it happened to me. Everyone knew a secret that I didn't know, and I spent all my mental energy coming up with every possible scenario and worrying about each one. No wonder Grandma would rather know right away.

God has a secret. He knows the outcome of your decisions. He knows if that date next week will lead to marriage, or if you will pass Organic Chemistry. It's in your nature, as a human and especially as a woman, to worry about these decisions. We would rather know right away, but within the waiting we learn to depend on God.

Learning to Trust

To illustrate this, let's carry the vaulting example a little further. When a gymnast runs toward the vault she builds up momentum. Jumping on the springboard creates an equal but opposite force upward. These accumulated forces give her the energy necessary to push off the vaulting horse and into some kind of dismount.

Of course, the gymnast controls many of these variables – how fast she runs, how effectively she pushes off the springboard, her form throughout, and how she encounters the vaulting horse. Once she gets to the vault itself, she can do a simple layout dismount or a complicated flip. The more skill and practice the gymnast has, the more options for dismounting, but these variables aside, natural constants like force and gravity make it all happen.

In the same way, you control many of the factors that lead to college, and the attitude with which you leave home emotionally and spiritually. You even control how you tumble over the precipice with your skills and practice. Do you want to merely graduate, or do you want to walk across that stage with medals around your neck? And like a gymnast knowing that gravity and physics will work for her, trusting God as you jump over the college precipice will bring peace and confidence throughout your academic career.

Concrete Steps for Trusting God

When faced with a decision, you can choose to make the decision ahead of God, or with God. Many people decide ahead of God, making up their minds long before they pray about it. Trusting God, though, means making decisions *with* God.

I have found that when I make a decision with God, the process follows these four steps. These steps don't come with a guarantee. God does as He pleases, whenever He wants; however He decides. We cannot manipulate Him. We can, however develop a profound confidence in His ability to care for us.

Step 1. Commit it to God in Prayer. Decide to let God decide. While you will be the physical being that literally says yes or no, pray for God to be the spiritual guide behind your answer. Doing this frees you from anxiety, because there's no need for worry when God leads.

In all decisions, pray for a clear sign either way – open doors to indicate that He wants you to do it, closed doors if He doesn't. Once you've prayed for God to lead in this area of your life, move on to the next step.

Step 2. Make *a* Plan. Gather as much information as possible. Do some research, compare prices, weigh the pros and cons. Opinions from level-headed friends and family members can also contribute to your plan – just make sure to keep their advice in perspective. In fact, try to keep the whole thing in perspective. Always be flexible when planning, and remember that God alone knows the best path.

Step 3. Work at it to the best of your ability. Do the work! Follow through on each step of your plan, leaving nothing undone.

Don't be lazy about achieving your goal. While God certainly can (and sometimes will) drop an opportunity directly into your lap, usually you must at least make some phone calls.

Step 4. Make a Decision. Take a deep breath. What feels like the natural answer? Go with your first instinct, then immediately pray for God to quickly change your mind if that instinct isn't right. Listen with your spiritual ear.

Then decide.

Practical Application

All of our God-is-like-gravity talk seems terribly abstract, however, when faced with a real-life decision. For example, let's say you want to find an internship in your desired field before junior year. What could you do to understand God's will about this internship?

Let's put these steps into action.

Step 1: Pray. From the moment the idea enters your head, begin praying. Initially, your prayer might be something like this: "God, you know about my goals to become an electrical engineer. Do you think an internship will get me to this goal? If this is the path for me, please show me the right choices to make in this direction. Please bring this opportunity into my life, and give me insight to see it. Help me avoid being distracted by lesser goals. If this isn't the path for me, close these doors. Amen"

Step 2: Plan. Early on you will need to gather as much information as possible about internships. Start with your academic advisor, then move on to the career center. Talk with professors, lab instructors, and fellow students. Pick up as much material as you can about becoming an intern, and research prospective companies.

Once you have a firm understanding of the process, write out the steps necessary to get the internship. Include names and numbers of people who have offered their help.

Through all of this, continue to pray for God's guidance.

Step 3: Work. Create a professional resume, possibly with help from the career center. Include everything that might be helpful. Ask for letters of recommendation from professors or previous employers who respect your work. Then send your resume to the correct person, whether through the college internship program or directly to the company.

Send follow-up emails to any relevant phone conversations. Complete any coursework that may be required. Pray continuously.

Step 4: Decide. Finally, after months (perhaps even a year or more) of working to find an internship, you now have two viable options: one in a large telecommunications company, the other in the repair division of an electronics retailer.

Thank God for blessing your efforts with these opportunities, and pray for His all-knowing hand to lead you. What seems like the best choice? Do you feel at peace with this choice? Pray for God to correct you if needed. Then decide.

He has walked with you the whole time, and He won't let you down at this crucial step.

God always keeps His word – when you committed the decision to Him at the very beginning of the process, He promised to lead you toward the right outcome. Remember the verse we opened with?

To man belong the plans of the heart, but from the Lord comes the reply of the tongue.

Chapter 8. Tools for Jumping

If God sends us on stony paths, He provides strong shoes. – Corrie Ten Boom

Pencils? Check.

Paper? Check.

Flip-flops for the dorm bathroom? Check.

Y ou could probably write a college prep essay in your sleep by now, and you don't need to be convinced that preparation leads to success. You already understand that studying for an exam will improve your score, and if the professor by some miracle gives an open-book exam, then you better make sure that particular book is in your backpack on exam day.

Like a good professor, God doesn't leave us hanging all by ourselves without a syllabus, textbook, or study group. As in the above quote by Corrie Ten Boom, He will provide the tools we need for difficult times, and if anyone ever understood difficult times Corrie Ten Boom would be that person.

The strange thing about life, even college life, is that we never know when our paved road might turn into a stony path. Everything could be wonderful, and then one day your best friend collapses into a drunken, suicidal depression in your bathtub, pulling the shower curtain rod on top of her as she falls. Someone close to you could die unexpectedly, or become addicted to meth, or be put in jail. A fellow classmate who seems disturbed and lonely could systematically murder 32 people on your campus. Life can become stony and painful in an instant.

So it would probably be a good idea to pack some strong spiritual shoes in your backpack next to the flip-flops and textbooks. It would be a better idea to put on those strong shoes right now.

Living and Active

Some professors only require one book. That one book could cost about $140, which you will pay through clenched teeth, throwing up your hands in frustration one month later when that same professor prefers to use his own class notes for exam questions. Other professors will require that you purchase six books, some large and some small. You might end up needing all these books, but more than likely you will only need a few paragraphs or chapters from each. With all this talk about books – literary books, text books, lab books, required books, recommended books, on-campus bookstores, off-campus bookstores, online bookstores – the most important book easily falls into the shadows.

Why wouldn't you want to spend time in the Word of God? Well….you're tired, too busy, or hungry. You already have a headache from reading all those required books. You have a booming social life. You need to wash your hair.

I can think of a few times in my life when I didn't want to read the Bible, and early college was one of them. I don't know why exactly, probably all of the above reasons plus a few more. Weeks would go by. Then months. Every now and then during that time I would crack it open, only to put it back in on my shelf a few minutes later. It didn't seem to apply anymore; it only reminded me of how far I had drifted.

For the word of God is living and active. Sharper than any double-edged sword, it penetrates even to dividing soul and spirit, joints and marrow; it judges the thoughts and attitudes of the heart. Hebrews 4:12

If I can't remember why I stopped reading the Bible, I remember even less why I began again. Guilt and grace during my wild oats phase gave way to renewed passion for God, and time in the Bible just came back naturally. Suddenly everything between its covers seemed relevant, because my soul thirsted for Truth. It became my life source, where I would find God even when my prayers felt empty.

Over time I realized that two things can shorten or prevent a spiritual dry spell in my own life. Reading the Bible consistently, regardless of whether it *feels* relevant, is the first one. The other is consistent prayer.

Prayer Without Privacy

Dorm life, student union activities, group meals, study groups, roommates, staying up until the wee hours – during college you will interact with your peers constantly. This interaction will help you understand various perspectives from people who lived differently than you. Maybe you grew up in a suburban, middle-class neighborhood, but your roommate went to school in the Bronx, walking through bad parts of town just to earn a high school diploma. Think of the conversations you might have, what you could learn from her, and she from you, but all this enrichment comes with a downside. You never have a moment for yourself! Hopefully you share a bathroom with only one other girl, but maybe you share a bathroom with the whole dorm floor. Sometimes even your private moments lose their privacy during college. Going into your own bedroom and closing the door for an extended prayer session just can't happen in most housing arrangements.

Christian colleges have the advantage in this arena. Roommates usually approach this issue on a level playing field, with mutual respect for each other's prayer needs. Even so, sometimes you just don't want anyone to hear your prayers. And that's okay – in fact, based on the following verse from Matthew, I think Jesus wants it that way: *But when you pray, go into your room, close the door and pray to your Father, who is unseen. Then your Father, who sees what is done in secret, will reward you.* Matthew 6:6

Through prayer, we talk with God in a most intimate fashion. We express emotions, thoughts, yearnings, disappointments – Jesus responds to these expressions with His own words, felt within our spirit. Bible studies and group worship certainly have their place, but no substitute exists for one-on-one time with the Father... *alone.*

In the Garden of Gethsemane, Jesus deliberately and unapologetically retreated away from His disciples to pray before the impending crucifixion. In Matthew 26:36, He says "sit here while I *go over there* and pray." He took Peter and the two sons of Zebedee, and said to them, "My soul is overwhelmed with sorrow to the point of death. Stay here and keep watch with me." Then in verse 39, "Going *a little farther,* He fell with His face to the ground and prayed."

Please notice something here. When Jesus talked with the Father, He did two things: 1) He separated completely from the larger group of fellow believers, and 2) He even went farther beyond a trusted few. While we know that Jesus drew strength from His disciples on a regular basis, at this moment of great distress and grief, Jesus wanted to be alone with His Father.

We need this same thing.

How Do I Find Privacy? Here's the key: take private moments with God when you can get them. Don't think to yourself – oh, I'll call my friend now, and wait until my next free moment to pray. That next free moment may be a week from now, and where will your walk with God be then?

So let's look at some examples of opportunistic God-moments.

Stoplight Prayers. If you drive a car, then you already have your very own private sanctuary. I personally like to pray while driving, but sometimes other drivers can distract me. God probably doesn't like me to yell, "hey, watch it, buddy!" during prayer time.

Teresa discovered a safer way to pray in the car.

"I remember in college, a friend of mine told me about 'stoplight prayers.' Basically, every time you stop at a stoplight, you are supposed to pray. The premise was that you would be following the passage that we are to 'pray without ceasing' and I found that it actually helped make my day brighter."

She adds, "Besides, what else is there to do while waiting for the light to turn green?"

Teresa learned how to take advantage of "downtime" moments for prayer. Even if the light turns green a few seconds after you start praying, you've made an effort to direct your thoughts toward God. Over time, stoplight prayers can translate into other areas – waiting for the coffee to brew each morning, walking to class, waiting for your computer to boot.

Letters to God. But what happens when you need an intense, prolonged prayer session, and you just can't get away from other people? Maybe you don't have a car. Maybe your roommate seems determined to never leave you alone, not even for a minute. Your soul cries out for alone time with God, but it just doesn't seem possible.

In these moments, you could express yourself by writing in a prayer journal. Janet, who attended a Christian university, remembers literally writing letters to God.

"One of the things that I remember doing to maintain my prayer life in college was to keep a prayer journal. I didn't just write items to pray over/about, but I actually wrote out my prayers. I wrote out sentences of praise, sentences of thankfulness, and sentences of requests to the Father."

Not only did prayer journaling help Janet maintain an intimate prayer life on campus, but it also helped her to stay focused.

"Doing that required me to spend time thinking about my prayer, and it kept me from falling asleep during my prayer," she says. "It helped me look at the language that I used to pray. I had to keep it real when I wrote it out. I don't think I used as many prayer clichés when I wrote it."

Strength in Numbers

Because Janet attended a Christian college that held regular chapel services, she also drew strength from worshipping beside her classmates and professors.

"I remember how helpful it was to attend special devotional times," she says. "Even when it was times of singing, it helped me focus on God which often led to prayer. Also, times of prayer with roommates, friends, boyfriend, etc. were good. It was an accountability measure, and helped me keep my eyes on the goal of being Christ-like."

If you go to a Christian college like Janet did, take advantage of every opportunity to share the Christian experience with others in your same peer group. And if you don't attend a Christian university, you will need to do two things: 1) find some Christian friends, possibly through a group like Campus Crusades for Christ; and 2) find and regularly attend a local church.

I don't think God meant for us to live the Christian life alone. Sure – if you were stranded on a deserted island you could still grow in your relationship with God simply by praying and reading the Bible. If you didn't have a Bible, memorized verses would come in handy. Aside from this extreme example, God created us to interact with each other, living out Christian love through serving and being accountable to each other.

Don't get me wrong – group worship cannot and should not replace *alone* time with God. But something miraculous happens when you pray and worship as a community, and I think it has much to do with love. Encouraging one another, praying for a friend, worshipping together – these things draw you into God's presence and out of your own problems. The empty, hurting, homesick parts of you will find supernatural healing, not only from God's work in your life, but though the community you find with fellow believers.

Let's just face it: even under ideal circumstances college can be a heart-wrenching, disturbing time and you will need encouragement. Those of you who grew up in a Christian home know what encouragement feels like. It's the uplifting word that helps you complete a project, the smile that provides hope, the shoulder to cry on, the soft words of truth when everything seems morally fuzzy. You may have received this kind of loving encouragement at home, and now you feel a sad void. Perhaps you have never known this type of support.

The encouragement you received at home represents a small portion of God's love for you. We learn how to use this love during fellowship with other believers.

Marcie went through a time during college when she didn't attend church, for fear of being called a hypocrite for her partying. As God brought her back, He showed her the importance of spending time with other Christians.

"I make sure that church is a priority at the top of my list," she says. "If want to go out on a Saturday night, I make sure to be home at a reasonable hour, so that I'll know I can wake up for church. Church is something I absolutely enjoy now, and I feel very deprived if I don't get to see and visit with my Christian brothers and sisters each week."

Going to a different church or returning to church after a long absence can be difficult, Marcie says.

"It may feel like a shock to your system at first, but just like any habit, going to church was something I had to get used to and just let it become a part of me."

Chapter 9. Becoming a (Godly) Confident Woman

The fact that I am a woman does not make me a different kind of Christian, but the fact that I am a Christian does make me a different kind of woman. For I have accepted God's idea of me, and my whole life is an offering back to Him of all that I am and all that He wants me to be. Elizabeth Elliot, in *Let Me Be A Woman*

This is the last chapter of our section entitled "Jumping." The first two chapters of this section focused on *what to do* as you jump over the college precipice from a faith perspective. In this chapter we're going to switch gears, and look not so much at *doing*, but at *being*. How should you be, as you jump into and over college? What spiritual character qualities should you have?

Those of you who grew up in church may feel tempted to skip this chapter. Please don't – it provides a backdrop for the final section of the book, a layer of information that will help frame some of the difficult subjects we must soon tackle together. Perhaps more importantly, it could positively change the way you view yourself as a Christian woman.

A large part of our world, even the Christian world, does not understand God-centered womanhood. Do you?

Pop Quiz: Please review the statements below and rate yourself on a scale of 1-5.

View of Women:

1	2	3	4	5

I am woman, hear me roar   *Women should keep silent*

View of Men:

1	2	3	4	5

A distraction   *"You complete me."*

View of Independence:

1	2	3	4	5

Self-support means everything   *I don't want to be alone*

View of God:

1	2	3	4	5

The Oppressor   *The Liberator*

Count your points. How did you score?

4-8: Women should be strong, independent, and free to
live as they please

9-15: Women should respect themselves, others, and
God

16-20: Women should be submissive, dependent on
others, and free from sin

Now take a minute to examine your feelings. Did anything about your own views surprise you? Pray for God to guide your heart. Before we move into this chapter, ask Him to tear down any prejudices, strongholds, and misconceptions that you may have about women, society, and Christianity itself. Have you done this? Then let's move on.

The Womanhood Gap

Churches believe that women (and men) should be Christ-centered, while culture teaches that women should be empowered. There doesn't seem to be a middle ground. But somewhere between Grr-l and Doormat there does exist a place where Godly women walk in confidence.

Yes, God wants women to be confident. No, He does not care which brand of deodorant you use. God's definition of confidence has nothing to do with superficial trust in the flesh. And that's where we begin to have trouble. We know what the world defines as a confident woman – we see that message on magazines, billboards, and television. But God probably does not rejoice when you wear a cleavage-baring dress, strutting your stuff in pride. So how might God define a confident woman?

Defining Confidence

Confident Woman (noun): She knows that God's spirit dwells within her, guiding her every step. This knowledge causes her to speak and act with authority within her own circle of responsibility, not with the power-driven authority the world seeks, but with steady assurance. Above all, she rests in her salvation through Jesus Christ.

You might say this is how God defines a confident *person*, male or female alike. But we've all read the passages: women should be silent in the churches and submissive to their husbands. Somehow, in the back corners of our minds, we've translated that to mean that women should yield all authority, all assurance. That interpretation isn't consistent with the rest of God's message to all of humanity.

Why shouldn't Christian women radiate confidence? As a child of the Lord Almighty, as a temple of the Holy Spirit, as one who sees and understands The Light in the midst of this dark world, God expects you to walk with confidence.

Godly Womanhood

So let's look at some biblical guidelines for Godly, confident women. I don't mean for this to be an all-conclusive list of Godly character qualities – I only want to highlight some areas that apply specifically to this current womanhood gap. Remember, this chapter focuses on being, rather than doing. Lots of books in the current market discuss what Christian women should do in the workplace, in the church, and in the home. But how should they be? What is the essence of how you should be?

We Should Be Fully Responsible for our Own Actions.

When Moses came down from Mount Sinai with the 10 Commandments, he then read them to all the Israelites – not just the men. From that point forward, God expected all men *and* women to keep his commandments. When Jesus died on the cross for the forgiveness of sins, He did it for everyone – male *and* female. Despite His own male-centered culture, Jesus viewed women as individuals, capable of coming to Him of their own initiative. If He really bought into the whole women-as-property notion, then He would have required women to get permission from their fathers or husbands before coming to worship Him. As you know, this isn't the case, and we each have a choice whether we accept that Jesus died to save us. On that day when you stand before God, and He asks you those two big questions – "What did you do with the life I lent to you," and "what did you do with My Son?" – your father, brothers, or husband cannot answer for you, just as you cannot answer for them.

We Should Both Give and Receive Respect.

In the Old Testament law, God commands us to "love your neighbor as yourself." Jesus takes this a step further, saying "you shall love your enemies and pray for those who persecute you" (Matthew 5:44). Love and respect go hand in hand, especially when talking about God's love, or agape love. Respect is "a feeling of deferential regard; esteem." Showing respect as defined here would certainly fall into the Christian love category – regard for a fellow human being. We should always employ a tone of respect in every area of life, including socially, academically, and professionally. By the same token, we don't need to go around demanding respect. This in itself does not respect others.

We Should Be Shrewd but Innocent.

Shrewd. In Matthew 10:16, Jesus says *"I am sending you out like sheep among wolves. Therefore be as shrewd as snakes and as innocent as doves."* Notice the phrasing that Jesus uses: "I send you out." He has a mission for you, and He wants you to be smart about it. Shrewd is defined as "characterized by keen awareness, sharp intelligence, and often a sense of the practical[8]." Something tells me that God doesn't want us women to be merely beautiful objects, walking naively through life as doormats for the whims of men (and other women). You should not blindly trust other people.

A shrewd woman would turn down a date with someone who literally looks her up and down before asking her out. She would learn how to handle her own business matters, taking down the first and last names of people who promise to do something for her, because without their names there would be no recourse within the company if this something doesn't get done. She would not be suspicious of those around her, but would take practical safety measures when out and about, such as parking under a streetlight at the mall. Should she feel called to minister on the streets of the inner city, she would dress modestly and she would not go alone. She uses common sense.

Innocent. But almost paradoxically, Jesus in the same breath says that you should be innocent. In all of your shrewdness, you shouldn't cross the line into sins like pride, arrogance, selfish ambition, empty arguments, or divisiveness. We have trouble with this one, because our culture teaches that pride and ambition will make you successful. Try to recognize the beginnings of pride or arrogance in yourself, especially when you begin to achieve your goals. Catching these sins early will keep them from growing into spiritual monsters.

A woman who finds this balance between shrewd and innocent would assertively express her case for being promoted at work, but she would stop short of comparing herself to fellow coworkers. She would carefully weigh her motives before entering into a debate of any kind, and if she found that she just wants to be right or respected, she would back down from the debate. She would not use others to get ahead.

We Should Be More Than Beautiful.

Proverbs 31:30 speaks directly to us women: "Charm is deceitful and beauty is vain, but a woman who fears the Lord, she shall be praised." Almost every woman falls into the beauty trap at least once in her life. What's so wrong with wanting to be beautiful or charming? Nothing, until it consumes your time, energy, money, and joy. But God needs you to keep the exterior package in perspective.

We Should Be Productive.

Proverbs goes on to say in verse 31:31: "Give her the product of her hands, and let her works praise her in the gates." Women should be able to work and receive favorable feedback about their efforts. By no means do these verses from Proverbs describe women as bimbos who need their husbands to think for them.

We Should Love God More than Anything Else.

When asked which commandment God considers to be most important, Jesus said "you shall love the Lord your God with all your heart, and with all your soul, and with all your mind. This is the great and foremost commandment" (Matthew 22:37-38). Notice something here: there's no room for selfishness. You can't hold part of yourself back – as in, "here, God, have this part of me, but I'm keeping my own goals no matter what You say." You also don't have room for loving someone or something else on an equal par with God – if placed in a position where you must choose between God or your boyfriend, or God and your best friend, or even God and your future husband, then you must choose God.

Trust plays a big role here – if you trust God with yourself and the people in your life, then those things will fall into place.

Chapter 10. Feminism and Your Future

You can't take up the cross until you've given up your right to yourself. Elisabeth Elliot

It's a great time to be a woman.

From politics to the corporate world, and just about everywhere in between, American women have more opportunities than ever before, certainly including your college campus. Since 1960, the female college population has almost doubled[9], with women now earning more degrees than men[10]. Career, purchase power, and R-E-S-P-E-C-T are all within reach, especially for a college-educated, forward-thinking young woman in today's society.

Why do you think we as a gender now have these opportunities? Is it because we are really that good?

Of course it is! But it's also because in the 1800s a group of political activists called feminists decided to change the world. I feel grateful for and humbled by their efforts, but unfortunately, feminism has changed through the years. Some argue that it evolved, but I disagree; what once provided freedom for women now promotes gender confusion and a rebellious attitude toward Godly life.

I'm going to be honest with you – I did not want to enter into the feminism debate when I began writing this book. The very thought of getting involved in such a heated topic makes my stomach hurt, but I can't get away from it. The feminist message thrives on college campuses, and like most secular philosophies, sifting out the good from the bad can be difficult.

A Brief History Lesson

First-Wave. The feminist movement officially began in the 1800's as progressive societies around the globe began to recognize that some cultures treated women unfairly, especially with respect to legal status and voting. These early efforts became known as first-wave feminism. For the most part, first-wave feminism freed women from true oppression, such as denial of full citizenship rights.

Susan B. Anthony, one of the most famous early feminists, said "[T]here never will be complete equality until women themselves help to make laws and elect lawmakers." By this definition, first-wave feminism was successful. We need only look at the women in the House, the Senate, and the 2008 presidential candidate list to know that this has been accomplished in our country, at least.

Second-Wave. When we hear and talk about modern feminism, we usually mean what's known as second-wave feminism, which began in the 1960's with bra burning (symbolic of freeing women from social constraints and inhibitions), birth control, and increased political pressure on government and corporations to treat women equally. In this era, women wanted professional equality in addition to legal equality.

The late Betty Friedan, a leading second-wave feminist, said "A woman is handicapped by her sex, and handicaps society, either by slavishly copying the pattern of man's advance in the professions, or by refusing to compete with man at all." Her message came across loud and clear: women should carry their own weight in the workplace and in society, and womanhood in itself shouldn't affect advancement or performance. While second-wave feminism did much to alleviate unfair treatment of women in a positive way, it also legalized abortion, increased divorce rates, and led to record numbers of children in childcare.

Third-Wave. The third-wave of feminism began in the 1990's and continues today. Within this third wave we've seen the rise of queer theory (the idea that we cannot compartmentalize people into labels like male, female, heterosexual, homosexual, and that these labels are socially constructed), and the new feminist agenda that takes feminism into all areas philosophical.

Judith Butler, a leading third-wave feminist philosopher, said "There is no gender identity behind the expressions of gender... Identity is performatively constituted by the very 'expressions' that are said to be its results." Basically, this means that gender *expression* determines identity, not actual gender, as in "I think I'm female, therefore I am female. And who are you to tell me I'm not female, despite what my anatomy says?" In this context it makes sense that third-wave feminism has strong ties with the gay rights community.

Feminism on Campus

From campus activists groups, to feminist professors, to people who don't think of themselves as feminists but unwittingly endorse the idea of gender relativity – you will undoubtedly run into third-wave feminist theory during your college career. And on the surface, it won't seem all that bad.

The largest feminist network, National Organization for Women (NOW), cites ending racism and violence against women among its top priorities. So sign me up – I don't want racism and violence either. Who can possibly say anything negative about such a goal?

At some point in your college career you will probably see a booth on your campus for the NOW campus division (Campus Action Network, or CAN). During January

2007 an article entitled "Young Feminists Mobilize College Campuses" appeared on the NOW website: "The University of Pittsburgh CAN... increased voter-turnout on their campus by 1,400 students. On Love Your Body Day, they scheduled on-site manicurists for anyone who wanted a little pampering around finals. They also provided a button-making machine so women could create their own sayings to express love for their bodies."

Increased voter turnout and Love Your Body Day sound pretty good to me. After all, female college students lead the pack for eating disorders and body image issues. Really, who can be against these goals?

But let's take a look at some of their other top priorities:

Abortion Rights/Reproductive Issues: "NOW fully supports access to safe and legal abortion, to effective birth control and emergency contraception [such as the "morning after" pill which prevents a fertilized egg from implanting in the uterine lining], to reproductive health services and education for all women."

Lesbian Rights: "NOW is committed to fighting discrimination based on sexual orientation or gender identity in all areas, including employment, housing, public accommodations, health services, child custody and military policies."

And take a look at this statement from the website for Campus Program of the Feminist Majority Foundation:

"The Feminist Majority Foundation (FMF) started the Campus Program to inform young feminists about the very real threats to abortion access, women's rights, affirmative action, and lesbian, gay, bisexual, and transgender rights posed by right wing extremists. FMF works with students on college campuses to affect change at the grassroots, national, and global levels."

This form of third-wave feminism confronts the very core of traditional Christian beliefs. Wherever you stand on the political scale, certain implications of the feminist movement can subconsciously chip away at your efforts to live a Godly life.

Understanding the Implied Message

For women, the philosophical feminist argument can be extraordinarily seductive. You may not label yourself a feminist, and you might never visit the NOW booth in your student union, but unless you "guard your hearts and minds in Christ Jesus," these ideas will infiltrate your thoughts and affect your future decisions.

Criticism of Patriarchy. The term *patriarchy* refers to a social system centered around fathers. Feminists regard patriarchy as an almost insurmountable problem in society. Most view the Bible as a source for unbridled patriarchal thought, since both the Old and New Testaments record mostly the actions of men, referring to women as "daughter of" or "wife of". And, as you know, the language of the Bible refers to God as male.

"Traditional" Women Have Been Brainwashed. Many feminist writers think that women who buy into the patriarchal system and choose traditional roles for themselves are victims of the patriarchal society. They believe these women are oppressed, and someday feminism will bring about their enlightenment.

Men and Women Are the Same. Despite a few anatomical differences (which can be changed if the heart wills it), feminists argue that men and women have essentially the same abilities, strengths, and weaknesses. Differences among the genders are only as real as culture defines them to be; feminists therefore focus much energy on changing cultural definitions.

Women are Entitled to _____. Because discrimination against women continues to run rampant, women must fight for the recognition and respect they deserve. Women have the right to put their needs and wants before the needs and wants of others.

Those Who Deny Us, Oppress Us. People or beliefs that encourage living within a framework of rules oppress the feminine spirit. Women should be free to make their own decisions in all areas of life (professionally, spiritually, sexually, morally) without facing judgment from others or life consequences such as unplanned pregnancy.

Some of your friends may be hooking up with guys left and right because they believe this message. They insist on the right to do what they want with their bodies, and nobody should say otherwise, but it will cost them – they will feel used even when they did the using, they will feel broken when they did the breaking. Our spiritual nature fights against these principles; God created humans to benefit emotionally from selflessness, not selfishness.

And unfortunately, worldly principles do their worst damage behind the scenes. By their very nature these ideas will affect future relationships, career path, marriage, the decision to have children, and parenting. Then there's the spiritual damage – how can you follow a God who oppresses women through patriarchy, denial of wants, and adherence to a specific feminine role?

Please don't let this philosophy set up camp in your being. Examine every thought that enters your head, every idea that pulls on your pride. Let the Holy Spirit heal the broken parts of your womanhood, which evil may have indeed oppressed. Our God sent His Son to die so that we might be free from such evil. He hates true oppression.

We need to remind ourselves that Jesus alone provides true freedom for *all* men and women.

In Chapter 9 we talked extensively about becoming a confident Christian woman. In this chapter we've grown aware that feminist philosophy can easily become ingrained even without that being our intent. In my opinion one reason Christian women struggle with confidence is because they have unknowingly adopted this philosophy, and they simply cannot reconcile the feminist view of self-centeredness with the Christian view of self-denial.

You may have noticed that this chapter ends in just a few more sentences. You won't find any solutions, no steps to overcoming feminist thought, no defensive arguments for the Christian viewpoint. Like me, you may feel emotionally and mentally drained from the hard work of sorting through this controversial issue, but take heart – we don't need to solve the world's problems on this page today.

Be aware; be on guard. And keep walking forward with God.

Chapter 11. Big Life Decisions

The secret is Christ in me, not me in a different set of circumstances. Elisabeth Elliot

You probably think about the future more often than you realize. How will you choose your major? By thinking about what type of career you want. How will you choose your career? By thinking about what you want to be doing in 10 years. Does this time frame include marriage, or even children? You will probably consider these questions in the back of your mind throughout college.

Because you will likely be stewing on these issues anyway, let's take some time to talk about them.

We all choose, one way or another, the paths we want to take in life.

For some people, life happens as if by accident. They drift here and there, in and out of marriages, not planning for the future in any way. They choose to live accidentally. For others, life happens on purpose. They make a plan and stick to it, for better or worse.

And then there's the third group. For this group, life deliberately happens according to God's purpose.

Deliberate life choices made *with* God lead to joy. People who live this way will not wake up one day and wonder why their lives don't work. If for some reason their lives stop working, they will know that God has a reason. They trust God's leadership.

Right now your life probably does not center on marriage and motherhood. You are more likely to worry about next week's test than something that may (or may not) happen years from now. While some of you will marry before you graduate from college; others will live the single life for a decade or more before settling down. So why think about any of it now? Why not deal with life as it happens?

Because what you think about now will become your future. The thoughts you have now about marriage, motherhood, and life in general will shape all those little small decisions you make along the way, leading to a lifestyle that reflects these thoughts. If you want to eventually become a Godly wife or mother you need to make some deliberate thought-choices along the way.

Thoughts about Marriage

Nobody can tell you who and when to marry but God Himself. You don't *really* know what will happen, even if you both have the best intentions and the most love that ever existed. More than half of all marriages end in divorce. Yes, even Christian marriages. You cannot know the future, nor can your best friend, mother, mentor, or fiancé. Only God really knows. Does this make sense to you?

Then why on earth do women often hold themselves to a plan they created as a preteen? "I plan to marry by age 28," or "I'll get married after medical school," or "I'm going to college to find a husband." When it doesn't happen that way, they become disappointed. Or they turn down that proposal from Mr. Right because they're not 27 and a half, and it's just not time yet.

When I met Brad after freshman year of college, the whole bells-and-butterflies thing happened. He was everything I wanted in a husband – great looking, a Christian, goal-oriented, and stable with money. It felt like we had known each other forever, like I found the missing puzzle piece. Like many women, though, I had a plan for how my adult life should proceed: enjoy myself during college, date for fun through my twenties, work hard at my career, and settle down by age 28.

So when Brad and I began talking about rings on a regular basis during sophomore year, part of me felt terrified. What did I do? I prayed like a madwoman, of course. My prayer went something like this: "God, this feels so right. But everyone else seems to think it's too early in my life. And we *are* so young, how can we know it will work?"

Literally on my face before God, I asked Him point-blank what I should do.

And get this: He answered me. I felt His answer as a peace in my spirit, and these words came to my head: you will marry Brad, and you will be happy.

Sure, my own plan changed – I fell in love with my husband almost 10 years ahead of schedule, but getting married young never happened accidentally for me. I made a deliberate choice to follow my own priority of being married, but on God's timeline rather than my own. We've been married for seven years now, and our joy in each other increases almost daily.

Not Me, We. Not that Brad and I don't argue or struggle with each other. We do. I have my own personality, and he has his, but our lives move forward as *we*. Not just him, not just me, but we.

Misty learned about this "we"-ness of marriage from her parents.

"My parents always gave the impression that they would rather be with each other than anyone else. Even now, they have a standing Saturday night date night that is pretty sacred," says Misty.

The model Misty saw growing up became the foundation for her own marriage to Justin, who she met during freshman year of college.

"My parents taught me to choose my husband over friends, family, even children. It is truly a covenant relationship. That means that I promised not only Justin but God to be with him only," Misty says. "I see it as the most important relationship I have, besides my relationship with God."

Respect. Something happened to us women in the past few decades – we want our men to respect us, and for the most part we want to respect them. But we really *don't know how* to respect them. Author Judy Carden provides her theory for this problem in her book, *What Husbands Need.*

"As women in this society, is it any wonder that the feminist notion that respect equates with weakness, subservience, and subjugation has affected us? Pay close attention to the next four or five articles you read in popular women's periodicals. How is the woman who is thoughtful, nurturing, and honoring of her husband portrayed?"[11]

Let's extend her discussion to television. Who really wears the pants, so to speak, in popular family sitcoms? In general, today's primetime shows portray husbands as ignorant, bumbling, self-absorbed adult children, while wives manage to run the house, raise the kids, have a career, and keep everything together.

These messages affect us dramatically, even when we know by now that art does not imitate real life. Sitcoms wouldn't be funny if everyone had it together. Women's magazines want to sell a message of empowerment and entitlement. Women buy this message, so they keep selling it.

Learn to recognize these destructive messages when you see them.

And ladies, if you want to enjoy a happy, healthy marriage someday, you must learn to respect your future husband now. Despite what we have learned from pop culture, he does not need a mother figure for a wife. He does not need to be manipulated into doing what you as his wife want him to do. He does not need to be trained, tolerated, or humored. He is not a big toddler who needs someone to shape his decisions and personality.

Of course, it doesn't take a college degree to know that a man does communicate differently than a woman. He needs someone who will try to understand these differences. He needs someone who loves him enough to overcome these communication barriers in search of true, deep communication. He needs someone to respect him as a man and as a human being regardless of his faults.

But people must earn respect, right? No, people must earn trust. Respect, on the other hand, comes from seeing people as God sees them. It seems so simple, but goes against everything in our culture: you need to respect your future husband because God created him worthy of your respect.

"It is when we look into our 'God heart'," writes Carden, "that we are able to see our husband with the value, attributes, and potential our Father sees in him."

Thoughts about Children

Children Should Change (Not Cancel) Your Goals. As women we instinctively know that motherhood will change us, but we too often take it to the next level – that mother-hood will *end* us. Why do we think this way?

Ladies, your future children will only be babies for a short time. Let me say without reservation that you need to be there. You need to be the one available for cuddles, kisses, and those first questions about God. But while you will always be their mother, you will not always be mothering. Those precious early years of cuddles and first questions end all too quickly. Full-time mothering only lasts for a season. After that season you will have increasingly more freedom to pursue other goals.

I would be in big trouble if life ended after having children, since I was 22 when my daughter was born. But God provided options for me, beginning long before I even thought about motherhood. During high school I couldn't decide if I wanted to become a journalist or a physician, as I'm passionate about both fields. But my college didn't offer journalism for a major, so I picked biology. Over time I realized that I didn't want to become a doctor. What, then, would I do with a biology degree?

Despite that question, I continued with my biology degree and loved every minute of it (well, almost every minute). I also worked for the school newspaper, and eventually found a job in health writing, not too far away from campus. Suddenly, I had found my career – a way to combine both of my passions. After college, I become the technical editor for a prestigious psychiatric medical journal, and traveled around the country to conferences with the nation's top psychiatrists.

When our first baby came along, I decided to stay home full-time, but we needed something to supplement our income. Thus I began editing and writing as a freelancer to bring in money. Now – another baby later – I do my writing and editing projects during the early mornings and when the kids go to preschool twice a week. I certainly accept much less work than before children, and I cut way back during the summer when they don't attend preschool. In this way, God has met our financial needs through my desire to stay at home *and* keep my professional foot in the door.

Your Children Deserve a Part of You. Sometimes women don't want their lives to change in any way – they want to have it all, without sacrificing anything of themselves. Becoming more domestic and maternal does not a modern woman make.

Mickey, for example, valued career over family for much of her young adult life.

"My primary concern was my career. I was very protective of anything that might infringe on my right to pursue a career as a modern woman," Mickey says.

While working throughout her twenties at a prominent pharmaceutical company, Mickey developed some strong opinions about marriage and children.

"There was no way I was going to let some man cow me into staying home with our children; fifty-fifty all the way," she says. "They would be his kids too, he should stay home as much as I should. All child rearing and housework would be split down the middle. I also was not going to drive a minivan."

When Mickey got married, she still felt ambiguous about children.

"I finally married a great guy who told me we could have kids, or not, whichever I wanted. I could stay home, or not, could even keep my maiden name, or not, whichever I wanted. I also continued my career," she says.

Mickey and her husband would soon learn that having a child does change things.

"Eventually, we decided we wanted to try a family. Everything went as planned, until we lost our first baby, our son, Ian, unexpectedly," she says. "That was when I realized I wanted to be all mommy to my babies. I was willing to trade my career for a healthy child, adopted or otherwise."

"Now, thanks to modern medicine, we finally have three little ones and I stay home to care for them, bake cookies and clean the house. I know this is what I need to be doing at this time in our lives and I'm very happy doing it."

"However, there are still no plans for a minivan in our future," she adds.

Despite what culture tells you, changing your goals because of motherhood does not make you weak. Women like Mickey are not letting down the team, so to speak. They are allowing a human connection, in fact the most basic human connection of mother and child, to motivate their actions.

Accountability

This world of husbands and babies and cookies probably seems overly burdened to you right now. You don't want to be tied down, responsible for the welfare of others. And you don't need to be – you should enjoy this freedom when you have it. All that other stuff will come later.

Right now you answer to yourself and God. Under this simple accountability system the future you will begin to take shape.

What does that person look like?

Chapter 12. A Woman Transformed

Only God can truly know our hearts, and thus only God can reveal our innermost selves to us. Penelope Stokes

Of all the struggles you will face in college and beyond, the most difficult one may be deciding what kind of woman you want to be. You don't just wake up one day with the ability to be Godly yet confident, shrewd yet innocent, or assertive yet humble. These attributes grow over time through little decisions you make on a daily basis. And while it would be wonderful if you could deliberately pick and choose your positive character traits, it doesn't usually work that way, at least not that easily.

Let's take the example of trusting God for guidance in decision-making. You grew up learning about God in church, about His miracles and love. You know that with God nothing is impossible. You want to be the kind of woman who trusts

God with everything, so why can't you seem to believe that God will solve your more concrete problems, like finding the right internship?

Lots of things can keep you from being the trusting person you want to become. Maybe somebody in your family betrayed your trust during childhood. Maybe as a teenager you allowed yourself to doubt God's existence, and the effects of this doubt linger today. Maybe you think that God doesn't care which path your career takes. Maybe, deep down in your subconscious, you don't want God to guide your future, because you're afraid that God's idea for your future won't make you happy.

We have so many ideals and imprints in our heads that compete with who we really are in God. These negative, often subconscious thoughts lead us to embrace character qualities that we don't want, which often don't fit our true identity. Unless you do something to counter these negative effects, the woman you eventually become will not be the one you want to be, nor the one God meant for you to be.

Authenticity

It's fine to talk about trusting God with choosing a major, or finding a job, but trusting Him with your identity? We would rather spend 15 minutes taking a Cosmo quiz about self-actualization, than allow God to make us authentic through 15 minutes of prayer.

Something that is authentic is the real thing, not fake. This is the first definition. But the second definition for "authentic" will give you chills: "having an origin supported by unquestionable evidence: *an authentic work by an old master.*" I'm not kidding – that's exactly what my dictionary says.

Your dreams, your self, *you* – these originated from the unquestionable hand of the Lord your God. If you allow it, this same hand will see His authentic work through to completion.

I have heard that the closer you come to God, the more you become yourself. It's a strange statement, because hopefully as you grow in faith, you become more like Christ as you let go of self. But somewhere in that transformation, *God brings you forth*, drawing out those wonderful unique qualities that make you who you are.

Sometimes this means recapturing traits lost during childhood and adolescence. Other times, like during the college years, this means allowing God to shape you even as other ideals try to shape you in their own way.

Authenticity means allowing God to make you spiritually real, by trusting Him to mold your identity, the very core of your being.

Entrusting Yourself to God

Let's take some time to examine this concept by using 1 Peter 4:19 as our guide. I love this verse, so I went ahead and used five translations. (I have underlined certain words from each – we'll talk about that in a few minutes).

So then, those who suffer according to God's will should <u>commit themselves</u> to their faithful Creator and continue to do good. (NIV)

Therefore, those also who suffer according to the will of God shall <u>entrust their souls</u> to a faithful Creator in doing what is right. (New American Standard)

Wherefore let them that suffer according to the will of God <u>commit the keeping of their souls</u> to him in well doing, as unto a faithful Creator. (King James Version)

So then, those who suffer because it is God's will for them, should by their good actions <u>trust themselves completely to their Creator</u>, who always keeps his promise. (Good News Translation)

So if you are suffering according to God's will, keep on doing what is right, and <u>trust yourself to the God who made you</u>, for he will never fail you. (New Living Translation)

In context, this verse follows a discussion about suffering as Christians, how we shouldn't be surprised or ashamed when we encounter suffering because of faith. Because we tend to think of such suffering as physical persecution

– a very real danger in Peter's time – we often have trouble relating this to our lives in America today.

Ladies, we all suffer to find ourselves in this fallen world.

Worldly ideals feed into our minds daily, affecting us like subliminal messages on a movie screen. We want to be strong, smart, independent, sexually confident, beautiful, perfect, nurturing, successful, thin, wealthy, and Godly, all at the same time. We carry emotional and psychological damage from our childhoods, we suffer to find the right path for our lives, we suffer to cope with disappointment, and we suffer loss. We suffer from the bad choices other people make. We suffer from our own spiritual blindness.

Sometimes this suffering boils to the surface, erupting as confusion, feelings of being torn, or just an intense sense of vulnerability. When this happens, you will encounter a spiritual fork in the road. During these times you decide who you are, and who you will become.

Our world contains far too many people who took the wrong way at these crossroad moments in their lives. They gave into selfish behavior and self-centered ambition. They took all that suffering and turned it either inward to themselves or outward to others. Peter suggests the better way – keep doing what is right, and trust God with all aspects of your being. He says that when things get crazy, when you're afraid you might actually go crazy, keep putting one foot in front of the other spiritually. Don't go off the deep end by responding to your suffering with sin.

And most importantly, *commit* those confused, torn, vulnerable parts of you to God.

We don't think much of commitment these days. Many of our earthly commitments can be broken with a word or some legal paperwork. You commit yourself to studying every afternoon until final exams, but break that commitment for a party. You entrust a secret to a friend, only to hear that secret circulating widely two days later. Committing yourself to someone seems good until the next thing comes along; you usually expect that people who have committed something to you may someday change their minds.

Fortunately, God takes commitment quite seriously.

In the verses above I underlined the phrases including the word *commit* or *entrust*. Please take a moment to review those verses, mentally emphasizing the phrasing. The original Greek uses the word *Parativqhmi*. In the context of this verse it translates to mean: to place down (from one's self or for one's self) with any one; to deposit; to entrust, commit to one's charge.

Jesus spoke this same word as he died upon the cross.

"Father, into Thy hands I <u>commit</u> My spirit."

So does God take you seriously when you *entrust* your identity to Him? Should you take Him seriously? Absolutely.

Upward and Onward

Throughout these pages we've described the college experience as a precipice, or situation of great peril. Graduating from college both academically and spiritually certainly constitutes a great life accomplishment – you've passed a myriad of tests, on all different subjects from a variety of sources. You've been stretched and strained, wounded and bruised, under-rested and over-caffeinated. You survived (even thrived) despite great peril.

When you graduate, the congratulations you receive will feel really good. And you will feel as though you have accomplished something wonderful, and you will have.

But a college degree doesn't make you any better.

Please read that last sentence once more.

Don't fall into the trap that Satan has set for educated people. What trap? The idea that you're better because you have a college degree. You may have more options, but college does not make you better than other people in the ways that really matter. As we read in 1 Corinthians, "Knowledge puffs up, but love builds up" (1 Corinthians 8:1). God would rather you be a loving, uneducated person than an arrogant erudite who can't (or won't) relate to others. I'm not saying that God doesn't want His followers to be educated, but knowledge without love is useless (1 Corinthians 13:2). You cannot truly love someone if you view yourself as better.

Beyond this precipice you will find another precipice, and then another, and others after that. They will be different for all of you. But with the arrival of every precipice, you will find God's hand ready to clasp yours. Imagine the freedom from worry, the lightheartedness. The peace. Can you feel it?

1. Costello RB (Ed.). (1991). *Random House Webster's College Dictionary.* New York, NY: Random House, Inc.

2. Longman K (2004). *Gender Issues Highlighted by CAP Findings.* Council for Christian Colleges and Universities. Last accessed February 25, 2008. http://www.cccu.org/resourcecenter/resID.2356,parentCatID.128/rc_detail.asp

3. Cook K (2004). *Women and Men Students in Christian College: Snapshots from the Assessment Data.* Council for Christian Colleges and Universities. Last accessed February 25, 2008. http://www.cccu.org/resourcecenter/resID.2357,parentCatID.128/rc_detail.asp

4. O'Malley PM, Johnston LD (2002). Epidemiology of alcohol and other drug use among American college students. *Journal of Studies on Alcohol* (Suppl. 14):23–39.

5. National Institute on Alcohol Abuse and Alcoholism (2002). Alcohol Alert No. 58: *Changing the Culture of*

Campus Drinking. National Institutes of Health. Last accessed February 25, 2008. http://pubs.niaaa.nih.gov/publications/AA58.pdf

6. College women who drink have an increased risk for sexual victimization. See: Gross WC, Billingham RE (1998). Alcohol consumption and sexual victimization among college women. *Psychol Rep* 82(1):80-82.

7. "Before the Throne of God Above", 2nd verse. Words and music by Charitie Bancroft and Vikki Cook.

8. The Free Dictionary. www.thefreedictionary.com/shrewd. Last accessed February 21, 2008.

9. Digest of Education Statistics (2004).

10. U.S. Department of Education, National Center for Education Statistics (2005).

11. Carden J (2006). *What Husbands Need: Reaching His Heart and Reclaiming His Passion*. Grand Rapids, MI: Kregel Publications.

12. Horton M, Byrd W (1984). *Keeping Your Balance*. Waco, TX: Word Books.

Printed in the United States
113176LV00004BA/88-90/P

9 781604 778465